परं सर्वात्मस्नपनं परं विजयते श्रीकृष्णसङ्कीर्तनम् सर्वात्मस्नपनं

बहुधा नाम्नामकारि बहुधा निजसर्वशक्ति- नाम्नामकारि नाम्नामका

नियमितः स्तत्रार्पिता नियमितः स्मरणे न कालःभगवन्ममापि स्तत्रार्पि

कृपा एतादृशी तव कृपा भगवन्ममापि भगवन्ममापि नाम्नामका

हाजनि दुर्दैवमीदृश... तव भगवन्ममाज्ञानन्दाम्बुधि

चेन तृणादपि सुनी... गना सहिष्णुना नाम्नामकारि

T0057359

नदेन अमानिना मानदेन कीर्तनीय सदा हरिः सदा आनन्दाम्बुधिव

न न स् न धनं न जनं न सुन्दरीं कामये कीर्तनीय सदा हरिः स्तत्र

गदीश कवितां वा जगदीशः कामये सदा जन्मनीश्वरे आनन्दाम्बुधि

जन्मनी मम जन्मनि जन्मनीश्वरे मां विषमे भवाम्बुधौ सदा ह

हेतुकी भवताद्भक्तिरहैतुकी त्वयिविषमे भवाम्बुधौभवताद्भक्तिरहैतु

ज! अयि नन्दतनुज! किङ्करं किङ्करं अयि नन्दतनुज!मम जन्मनि

षमे पतितं मां विषमे भवाम्बुधौ मां विषमे भवाम्बुधौ सदा हरि

पद कृपया तव पादपङ्कज- अयि अयि निश्चिन्तय

मस्तपनं परं विजयते श्रीकृष्णसङ्कीर्तनम् सर्वात्मस्नपनं सर्वात्म

मकारि बहुधा निजसर्वशक्ति- नाम्नामकारि नाम्नामकारि नाम्नामव

र्पिता नियमितः स्मरणे न कालःभगवन्ममापिस्तत्रार्पिता स्तत्रार्पि

शी तव कृपा भगवन्ममापि भगवन्ममापि नाम्नामकारि एतादृशी

मीहशमिहाजनि नानुरागःतव भगवन्ममाज्ञानन्दाम्बुधिव दुर्दैवमीह

रपि सुनीचेन तरोरिव सहिष्णुना सहिष्णुना नाम्नामकारि तृणादपि

निना मानदेन कीर्तनीय सदा हरिः सदा आनन्दाम्बुधिव अमानिन

नं न जनं न सुन्दीं कामये कीर्तनीय सदा हरिः स्तत्रार्पिता न धनं

तां वा जगदीशः कामये सदा जन्मनीश्वरे आनन्दाम्बुधिव कवितां

जन्मनि जन्मनीश्वरे मां विषमे भवाम्बुधौ सदा हरिः मम जन्

द्भक्तिरहेतुकी त्वयिविषमे भवाम्बुधमैवताद्भक्तिरहेतुकी भवताद्भ

नन्दतनुज! किङ्करं किङ्करं अयि नन्दतनुज!मम जन्मनि अयि न

मां विषमे भवाम्बुधौ मां विषमे भवाम्बुधौ सदा हरिःपतितं म

न तव पादपङ्ज- अयि अयि विचिन्तय आनन्दाम्बुधिव कृपया

Bhajan

Mantras of Mercy

MANDALA
PUBLISHING

Your Publisher for Life

354 Bel Marin Keys Blvd., Suite D

Novato, CA 94949

t. 415.883.4055, f. 415.884.0500

info@mandala.org, www.mandala.org

For orders or free catalog, call 800.688.2218

ISBN: 1-886069-83-2

Designed and printed by Palace Press International

www.palacepress.com ● Printed in China

Bhajan

Mantras of Mercy

Text by Swami B. B. Tirtha & Swami B. V. Tripurari

MANDALA
PUBLISHING

Contents

Introduction

By N.D. Koster

Bhajan is a celebration of Bengali devotional songs that sprang from the Bhakti Yoga renaissance inspired by Chaitanya Mahaprabhu in the 15th century. Traditional melodies reinterpreted by Rasa offer sublime, soothing accompaniment to truly transformational mantras of mercy. The chanting of these sacred syllables and songs, each pregnant with knowledge of the Absolute, reaffirms the relationship between divinity and soul. *Bhajan* invokes the holy names of Krishna, Madhava, Keshava, Gopal and Govinda, singing to us of the power in sound, the divinity in God's name, and love's power to conquer all.

Articles by Swami B. B. Tirtha and Swami B. V. Tripurari, both modern day representatives of Chaitanya's teachings, provide a penetrating glimpse into the Vedic worldview and its practical application in our daily lives. Their writings, both intimate and instructional, provide an abundance of inspiration along with historical context for those new to the practice of chanting. The authors' words confirm that the rising interest in the subject is much more than a fad or curiosity about world music; indeed, the holy names themselves are divine. Brimming with transcendental potency, they draw each singer closer to a living wisdom within.

I know not how thou singest, my master! I ever listen in silent amazement. The light of thy music illumines the world. The life-breath of thy music runs from sky to sky. The holy stream of thy music breaks through all stony obstacles and rushes on. My heart longs to join in thy song, and I cry out baffled. Ah, thou hast made my heart captive in the endless meshes of thy music, my master!

—RABINDRANATH TAGORE, *Gitanjali*

7

Days come and ages pass, and it is ever he who moves my heart in many a name, in many a guise, in many a rapture of joy and of sorrow. —RABINDRANATH TAGORE, *Gitanjali*

Chanting in the Age of Kali

By Swami B. B. Tirtha

Many cultures divide time into four eras: the Golden Age, Silver Age, Bronze Age and Iron Age. In the Vedas these are referred to as Satya-yuga, Treta-yuga, Dwarpa-yuga, and Kali-yuga. Time is understood to revolve in cycles, from Satya-yuga to Kali-yuga, over and over again.

In these ages, or *yugas*, we see the gradual deterioration of humanity from happiness and innocence to sorrow and ignorance. The most degraded condition exists in the present age of Kali-yuga, the Iron Age. According to Vedic scripture, in this dark time, people are characterized by a lack of ethics and compassion. It is an age of quarrel and hypocrisy. Therefore it is very difficult to find a legitimate spiritual guide, or even truly spiritually motivated people.

Krishna saw the plight of the human beings in Kali-yuga. He saw a time with no saints, no gurus. So He Himself incarnated as Chaitanya Mahaprabhu in the year 1486 in West Bengal, wrapping Himself in the golden complexion and worshipful mood of Radharani, His absolute counterpart and most devoted. In this way He gave a special blessing to the people of Kali-yuga, offering them a connection with divinity through *sankirtan*, the chanting of the Holy Names, and reestablishing the Bhakti Yoga tradition in modern times through His successors.

Chaitanya Mahaprabhu taught that the root cause of our affliction is forgetfulness of our relationship with divinity. In remembering Krishna we are freed from all afflictions and shielded from the unholy influence of this age. But how can this be accomplished? In Kali-yuga the practice of meditation will not be successful because our minds are restless. The mind is always jumping here and there like a monkey. How can we meditate nowadays? So many worldly things will come to our mind. By closing our eyes we are not truly meditating. We close our eyes and end up in London! As we are given the things of this world through the senses, those same things will enter into the mind. The mind is a storehouse, and every time we try to meditate many thoughts will bombard us.

In Satya-yuga meditation was possible. The people of that age had purity, compassion, and respect for truthfulness. But when these qualities degenerated in Treta-yuga, it was no longer possible to strictly meditate on the Supreme Lord. At that time the sages prescribed *yajña*, or sacrifice. Later, in Dwarpa-yuga, people couldn't pronounce the mantras prescribed by the Vedas correctly. So the sages and scriptures prescribed worship of the deity form of the Lord. In deity worship, one must concentrate in order to be successful, and all the senses must be engaged in the service of the deity. But in Kali-yuga, this is not possible. People in Kali-yuga have very fragile physical and mental health, and the Vedas actually prohibit such people from conducting worship. We are all diseased in this way though, so what can we do? Krishna's response has come through Chaitanya Mahaprabhu; "You can perform *Harinam sankirtan*. You can chant the Holy Name. I shall appear as Harinam [My name] in this world and give all power to it."

What then is the meaning of sankirtan? It means to sing and chant about the transcendental glories, names, forms, attributes, and pastimes of Krishna entirely, only, exhaustively and fully. For that reason Chaitanya Mahaprabhu has taught us how to perform Harinam sankirtan. He said we should be more humble than a blade of grass, more tolerant than a tree, offering respect to all others without demanding any respect for ourselves. If we chant the Holy Name with this attitude we will achieve our eternal welfare. Then we will know that we are of Krishna, that we are His eternal servants, and that that is a glorious position. To accomplish this we must chant from the core of our hearts.

By chanting the Holy Name you can attain the highest goal. In Kali-yuga, truth is found in the Holy Name. Krishna appears here as his name, so take shelter here. The name of Krishna and Krishna himself are the same. It is not a material or mundane sound. In material sound, you will find the thing referred to by sound is different from the sound itself. The word "water" is different from the substance we call water. The word refers to a thing understood to be water. By uttering "water" we cannot quench our thirst. But Krishna and the name of Krishna are one and the same. Chaitanya Mahaprabhu wrote:

> Throughout the whole world there is a forest fire. Everyone is suffering under their own false ego: they think they belong to this world. Utter Krishna's name from the core of your heart. You will get everything. Your mind will be sanctified and all your difficulties will be removed.

This is the first attainment of chanting. If we come to love Krishna, then we see every living being in relation to Him. Then we can love naturally, because we see everything and everyone in relation to the center. Parents are not taught to love their child. They love automatically due to relation.

In Goloka Vrindavan where Krishna resides, the inhabitants are drowned in bliss. At every step they experience the sweetest ever-increasing ecstasy, because everybody's motivation is to satisfy Krishna. The center is one. If you draw different circles with one center, there will be no crossing. But if there are different centers, the circles will cross and lines will clash. As long as there are different groups and different centers, we cannot stop fighting in this world. We should stop thinking that we are the center. The chanting of the Maha Mantra and Harinam sankirtan extinguishes this forest fire.

By chanting the Holy Name you can attain the highest goal.

The Efficacy of Sound and the Divinity of Krishna's Name

By Swami B. V. Tripurari

We have heard that *bhajan* and *kirtan*—congregational singing of the names of God—are very effective for people in the time of Kali-yuga. This is not a sectarian statement, but rather Chaitanya Mahaprabhu's emphasis on universal principles regarding the potency of sound and the divinity of God's name. These principles are acknowledged in both the religious and secular worlds.

> *I feel that the ferry of my songs at the days end will bring Me across to the other shore from where I shall see.*
>
> — RABINDRANATH TAGORE, FIREFLIES

If we examine how the name of God is thought of in all religious traditions and how sound is important to us in everyday life, then we can better appreciate the universality of the precept that Chaitanya Mahaprabhu sought to drive home, making it the central

15

इन्द्र शर्मा.

focus of His time on earth. By looking deeply into Mahaprabhu's emphasis, we will also find another universal principle: love's power to conquer all. In Mahaprabhu's teaching, this includes even God Himself.

Sound is an element that the modern technological world has under utilized in comparison to fire, water and earth. Perhaps this is yet to come, because it is clear that the potential power of sound is tremendous. Our mind, for example and in a very basic sense, functions in terms of acceptance and rejection, and each of these is driven by sound. Sound helps our mind put thoughts into ideas, as well as dismantle them. The entire mental system of every individual is profoundly affected by what one hears and speaks.

Chaitanya Mahaprabhu understood the influence of sound very well. The Vedic sages also thought about it deeply. Members of the Vaishnava tradition say that seeing is really about hearing. *Darshan*, or seeing, is related to hearing. It is said that the Vaishnava sees with his ears because his vision is guided by the sounds of the scripture. According to the Vedic scriptures, the entire material world is a product of sound.

Sages concluded that the world comes from sound and that material existence can also be retired by sound. In fact, *Vedanta-sutra* finishes with the words *anavrittih sabda anavrittih sabda*. This means that going beyond material existence, one never returns. Why is this so? Because of the word, because of the sound, or scriptural evidence,

which says as much. This sound, the scriptural evidence, is difficult to understand. In Srimad Bhagavatam it is stated:

The spiritual sound of the Vedas is very difficult to comprehend. It manifests within the life air, the senses, and the mind. This Vedic sound is unlimited and unfathomable, just like the ocean.

(11.21.36)

We can only hope to understand the scope of Vedic wisdom through submissive hearing of its sounds, and by hearing repeatedly from the proper source. Hearing and chanting the Vedic sounds repeatedly will create a spiritual impression on our consciousness leading to a comprehensive understanding of the nature of reality.

We are all moving in the world based on certain impressions. These impressions are called *samskaras*. A rope, rubbed once across a stone, makes no impression. But after grazing the stone many times, the

rope creates friction and starts to make a mark on the stone. Over time, repeated impressions make us prone toward one thing or the other. Impressions from previous lives cause us to move in a particular way, to have a particular tendency, or appreciate a particular type of music and so forth.

By the influence of Vedic sound, two things gradually happen: our previous samskaras are nullified and a sobering impression is created whereby we can see clearly. At the time of spiritual initiation a samskara for *bhakti* (devotion) is created. To further nourish that impression, instruction is given with considerable emphasis on repetition of the name of God.

Among Vedic sounds the name of God has been given enormous emphasis. Rupa Goswami, a 15th century Vaishnava scholar and poet who studied under Mahaprabhu, has stated in the first verse of his *Namastakam* that the root of the *sruti*, the core text that comprises the essential *Upanishads*, has been compared to a garland of gems, and these gems are giving off light. Where are they shining that light? They illumine the Holy Name of Krishna. The Vedas are very broad in their scope of knowledge and comprise a jungle of sounds. On which sounds shall we focus our attention? Of all sounds, the sound consisting of the name of God is most efficacious, and according to Chaitanya Mahaprabhu, of all God's names "Krishna" is most glorious.

The religious world is familiar with the idea that the name of God has power. The Greek term "theology" was originally intertwined with the divinity in the names of God. In our times, theology has come to mean a kind of divine science, the logic (logica) of divinity (theo). But previously it was used in relation to names of gods. The Greeks had many gods, and they had a particular type of person who was designated for calling the names of the gods. This person was called a theologian. He would call specific names at specific times to invoke the influences of specific gods for specific purposes. In many respects this was the sum and substance of what religion involved for the Greeks.

ॐ दयायुनाय नमः

ॐ विघ्ननाशनाय नमः

The Greeks had many gods, and they had a particular type of person who was designated for calling the names of the gods. This person was called a theologian. He would call specific names at specific times to invoke the influences of specific gods for specific purposes.

Even in the secular world, names have power. In previous times, people wouldn't give out their name very easily. Nowadays this is also true, but names have been replaced in the United States with Social Security numbers. People don't give out their Social Security numbers very easily because they run the risk of being controlled by those who know it. If someone knows your Social Security number, they can find out everything about you. Numbers have replaced names, but the principle is the same: By knowing the name of a person, you can know everything about him. This is what Chaitanya Mahaprabhu taught with regard to the Holy Name of Krishna and Krishna Himself. The two, name and named, are one. Truly knowing His name, one knows Him.

Among the various saints in the 15th and 16th century India there was a reaction to the so-called *smarta* monopoly on salvation that mandated one must first be born in a Brahmin family and then accept *sannyas*, the renounced order of life, before attaining salvation. There was a rebellion against this philosophy; the idea that God was actually more accessible to the common people challenged the status quo. The Bhakti movements championed this. They voiced this with emphasis on God's name. Nanak, Kabir, and others placed great emphasis on the name of God as a means to salvation. They saw the names of God— Hari, Rama, Krishna—to be a means of attaining the nameless status of Brahman. Nothing was more important to Kabir in terms of spiritual practice than the name of Rama. Guru Nanak emphasized *sat-nama*, and his scripture is filled with glorification of the names of Rama and Krishna.

Shining out among these religious traditions came Chaitanya Mahaprabhu's conception of the name of God. Mahaprabhu was the most prominent advocate of devotion and chanting of the time. He made a *dharma*, a religion, out of the name of God. His followers developed this idea in great detail, and thus we have a theology of the Holy Name, *nama-dharma*. The significance of this nama-dharma and the ontological position of Krishna's name were revealed over time through the realizations of the devotees of Chaitanya Mahaprabhu.

At first the name of Krishna was considered to be the avatar of God in syllables. This insight was one in which it was considered that the syllables *krs* and *na* were empowered with the potency of God, making Krishna's name an empowered incarnation of Himself. But gradually this insight was surpassed by the realization that Krishna and His name were one and the same.

How much further can we go in glorifying the position of the name of Krishna? Rupa Goswami has gone even further. The Name and Named are non-different, but if we look more closely we find that there is also a difference. The Name is more merciful than the Named.

Sometimes people say "Oh, Chaitanya Mahaprabhu came five hundred years ago;

Krishna came five thousand years ago. If only I was there then, how fortunate I would be!" But they've missed the point: The Name is here now. It has been given to us. If we chant the Holy Name with this attitude then our fortune will be great.

We are accustomed to making things part of our agenda, pulling them out of our pocket to support our mentally conceived cause. We should not attempt this with the name of Krishna. We gather knowledge to further our agenda, but this name embodies a different kind of knowledge. It is of a different nature altogether. It has its own very high agenda, and our soul is on it.

Mahaprabhu said that the mantras of the *Upanisads* are very far from actual talk of Krishna. What can happen from saying "*aham brahmasmi*," or "*tat tvam asi*"? What kind of change in our life can come from that? There will be some transformation, but it will not be as comprehensive as that which chanting the Holy Name can bring about. By the mercy of this chanting we can exit the world of birth and death and enter the world of ecstasy. Mahaprabhu taught that the transformation brought about by chanting is far-reaching, and moreover, there are no rules attached to chanting the holy name of Krishna. So many rules are attached to the chanting Vedic mantras, but Krishna is distributing Himself freely through His name proportionate to our faith in Him, a faith that He Himself has awakened.

Rupa Goswami described Chaitanya Mahaprabhu walking to Puri holding a knotted string, counting each knot and loudly chanting the Maha Mantra, Hare Krishna Hare Krishna Krishna Krishna Hare Hare Hare Rama Hare Rama Rama Hare Hare.

This nama mantra is also mentioned in the Upanishads:

iti sodasakam namnam kali-kalmasa-nasanam
natah parataropayah sarva-vedesu drsyate

hare krishna hare krishna
krishna krishna hare hare
hare rama hare rama
rama rama hare hare

This mantra is so pleasing
of His dearmost, Sri Radha, but also of Her
to Krishna because it speaks not only
power to subjugate Him.

All the Vedas say this arrangement of God's names is most beneficial for Kali-yuga. This emphasis comes with good reason. What is the secret behind this mantra? The Maha Mantra speaks indirectly, secretly, of something very sweet. "Hare" means *Hari* in the vocative. "O Hari, O Krishna, O Rama." But the Gaudiya lineage has analyzed this further, and they have concluded that "Hare" also means *Hara*, a name for Radha in the vocative. Indirectly the divine union of Radha and Krsna is the subject of this mantra. Here the names "Rama" and "Krishna" are surrounded by "Hare," (Radha), on all sides. "Krishna" means Krishna, and "Rama" is another name for Krishna (*Ramana*). Radha is "Hare," she who steals away Krishna's mind.

This mantra is so pleasing to Krishna because it speaks not only of His dearmost, Sri Radha, but also of Her power to subjugate Him. The name Hare announces this. When Krishna hears us chant this He will say, "You know that about Me, that I am subjugated by Her influence? I am the Supreme God, yet she can turn me into a dancing madman! You know that she is My guru?" Krishna will want to silence us if he hears us sing this secret mantra loudly by taking us to his abode.

Such is the glory of the Maha Mantra and the precept of Sri Chaitanya Mahaprabhu. It speaks to us of the power in sound, of the divinity in God's name, and of love's power to conquer all.

Narottam Das Thakur

Narottama Das Thakur lived in the 16th century, in the period immediately following the disappearance of Chaitanya Mahaprabhu. As such, he is considered one of the leaders of the second generation of Gaudiya Vaishnavas. Narottam's name is usually associated with those of Shyamananda Prabhu and Srinivas Acharya, as these three great saints were among the first Bengalis to go to Vrindavan in the post-Chaitanya period in order to study the teachings of the Six Goswamis under Sri Jiva Goswami. On completing their studies, they returned to Bengal, where they popularized these teachings, especially through the medium of song, or kirtan. Narottama Das in particular composed many songs, collected as *Prarthana* ("Prayers") and *Prema-bhakti-candrika* ("The Moon-rays of Loving Devotion"), which remain the essential prayer books of all those who follow the Gaudiya Vaishnava tradition.

DEVOTION

Vishwanath Chakravarti Thakur

Born in Bengal in the mid-17th century, Vishwanath Chakravarti became the most prominent *acharya* of the Gaudiya Vaishnava school after Rupa Goswami himself. A prodigious scholar, Vishwanath wrote primarily in Sanskrit; his prolific output includes numerous commentaries as well as original works of poetry and theology. His theological writings helped resolve many controversies that arose during his lifetime. He also wrote many songs in the Bengali language.

Vishwanath's poetic sensibility gave him a unique and delightful vision of the Goswamis' teachings and his original descriptions of Radha and Krishna's pastimes, like *Prema Samputa*, *Krishna Bhavanamrita* and *Chamatkara Chandrika*, are a joy to all devotees. He left this world in the early 17th century in Vrindavan.

Songs & Translations

Kabe Habe Bolo

"When Will that Day be Mine?"

Written by Bhaktivinode Thakur, Bengali, 19th century

kabe ha'be bolo se-dina āmār
aparādha ghuci, śuddha nāme ruci
kṛpā-bale ha'be hṛdoye sañcār

tṛṇādhika hīna, kabe nije māni
sahiṣṇutā- guṇa hṛdoyete āni
sakale mānada, āpani amānī
hoye āswādibo nāma rasa sār

dhana jana āra, kobitā sundarī
bolibo nā cāhi deha sukha-karī
janme janme dāo, ohe gaura hari
ahaitukī bhakti caraṇe tomār

korite śrī-kṛṣṇa- nāma uccāraṇa
pulakita deho gadgada bacana
baibarnya- bepathu ha'be saṅghaṭana
nirantara netre ba'be aśru-dhar

kabe nabadwīpe, suradhunī-taṭe
gaura nityānanda boli niṣkapaṭe
nāciyā gāiyā, berāibo chuṭe,
baṭulera prāya chariyā bicār

When Will that Day be Mine?

When, O when, will that day be mine? When will you give me your blessings, erase all my offenses and give my heart a taste for chanting the Holy Name in purity?

When will I taste the essence of the Holy Name, feeling myself to be lower than the grass, my heart filled with tolerance? When will I give respect to all others and be free from the desire for respect from them?

When will I cry out that I have no longer any desire for wealth and followers, poetry and beautiful women, all of which are meant just for bodily pleasure? O Gaura Hari! Give me causeless devotional service to your lotus feet, birth after birth.

When will my body be covered with goose bumps and my voice broken with emotion as I pronounce Krishna's name? When will my body change color and my eyes flow with endless tears as I chant?

When will I give up all thought of the world and society to run like a madman along the banks of the Ganges in Nabadwip, singing and dancing and sincerely calling out the names of Gaura and Nityananda?

When will Nityananda Prabhu be merciful to me and deliver me from the enchantment of the sense objects? When will he give me the shade of his lotus feet and the right to enter the marketplace of the Holy Name?

Srila Bhaktisiddhanta Saraswati Thakur ~ One of the Great Gurus of the Gaudiya Tradition

Sri Sri Guruvastaka

Also known as Samsara Prayers

"Hymn to the Spiritual Master"

WRITTEN BY VISHWANATH CHAKRAVARTI THAKUR, SANSKRIT, 17TH CENTURY

saṁsāra-dāvānala-līḍha-loka-
trāṇāya kāruṇya-ghanāghanatvam
prāptasya kalyāṇa-guṇārṇavasya
vande guroḥ śrī-caraṇāravindam

mahāprabhoḥ kīrtana-nṛtya-gīta-
vāditra-madyan-manaso rasena
romāñca-kampāśru-taraṅga-bhājo
vande guroḥ śrī-caraṇāravindam

śrī-vigrahārādhana-nitya-nānā-
śṛṅgāra-tan-mandira-mārjanādau
yuktasya bhaktāṁś ca niyuñjato 'pi
vande guroḥ śrī-caraṇāravindam

śrī-rādhikā-mādhavayor apāra-
mādhurya-līlā-guṇa-rūpa-nāmnām
pratikṣaṇāsvādana-lolupasya
vande guroḥ śrī-caraṇāravindam

yasya prasādād bhagavat-prasādo
yasyāprasādān na gatiḥ kuto 'pi
dhyāyan stuvaṁs tasya yaśas tri-sandhyaṁ
vande guroḥ śrī-caraṇāravindam

S O N G S & T R A N S L A T I O N S

Sri Sri Guruvastaka

The spiritual master is receiving benediction from the ocean of mercy. Just as a cloud pours water on a forest fire to extinguish it, so the spiritual master delivers the materially afflicted world by extinguishing the blazing fire of material existence. I offer my respectful obeisances unto the lotus feet of such a spiritual master, who is an ocean of auspicious qualities.

Chanting the Holy Name, dancing in ecstasy, singing and playing musical instruments, the spiritual master is always gladdened by the sankirtan movement of Lord Chaitanya Mahaprabhu. Sometimes his hair stands on end, he feels quivering in his body and tears flow from his eyes like waves. I offer my respectful obeisances unto the lotus feet of such a spiritual master.

I worship the lotus feet of the spiritual master, who is engaged in regularly worshiping the Lord's deity form by dressing Him and serving Him in other ways, by washing the temple and so on. Not only is he so engaged, but he engages his students in these same activities.

I offer my respectful obeisances to the lotus feet of my spiritual master, who is filled with enthusiasm for relishing at every moment the unequalled sweetness of Radha and Krishna's pastimes, qualities, forms and names.

By pleasing the spiritual master, one pleases the Supreme Personality of Godhead; whereas displeasing him means that one has no chance of making spiritual progress. One should therefore meditate and pray for his mercy three times a day. I offer my respectful obeisances unto the lotus feet of my spiritual master.

Nama Sankirtan

Also known as Hari Haraye

"A Song of Krishna's Names"

Written by Narottam Das Thakur, Bengali, 16th century

hari haraye namaḥ kṛṣṇa yādavāya namaḥ
yādavāya mādhavāya keśavāya namaḥ
gopāla govinda rāma śrī-madhusūdan
giridhārī gopīnātha madana-mohan
śrī-caitanya-nityānanda śrī-advaita-sītā
hari guru vaiṣṇava bhāgavata gītā

Nama Sankirtan
TRANSLATION

Obeisances unto Lord Hari
Obeisances unto Krishna known as Yadava
(best of the Yadu dynasty)
unto Madhava, the husband of the goddess of fortune,
unto Keshava, he of fine hair,
Gopala, the cowherd boy,
Govinda, the pleaser and protector of cows,
Rama, the reservoir of pleasure,
Sri Madhusudan, the killer of the demon Madhu,
Giridhari, the lifter of Govardhana hill,
Gopinath, Lord of the cowherd damsels,
Madan Mohan, the enchanter of Cupid,
To Lord Chaitanya (the incarnation of mercy)
to Nityananda and associates,
and to the Srimad Bhagavatam and Bhagavad Gita.

Sri Rupa Manjari Pada

Also known as Sri Rupa Manjari

"Rupa Manjari, Eternal Maidservant of Lord Krishna"

BY NAROTTAMA DAS THAKUR, BENGALI, 16TH CENTURY

śrī rūpa mañjarī pada   sei mora sampada
sei mora bhajana-pūjana
sei mora prāṇa-dhana sei more ābharaṇa
sei mora jīvanera jīvana

sei mora rasa-nidhi sei mora vāñchā-siddhi
sei mora vedera dharama
sei vrata, sei tapa sei mora mantra japa
sei mora dharama karama

anukūla habe vidhi se pade haṅbe siddhi
nirakhibo ei dui nayane
se rūpa mādhurī rāśī prāṇa kuvalaya-śaśi
praphullita habe niśi-dine

tuwā adarśana ahi garale jārala dehi
ciradina tāpita jīvana
hā hā prabhu koro dayā deha more pada chāyā
narottama laṅla śaraṇa

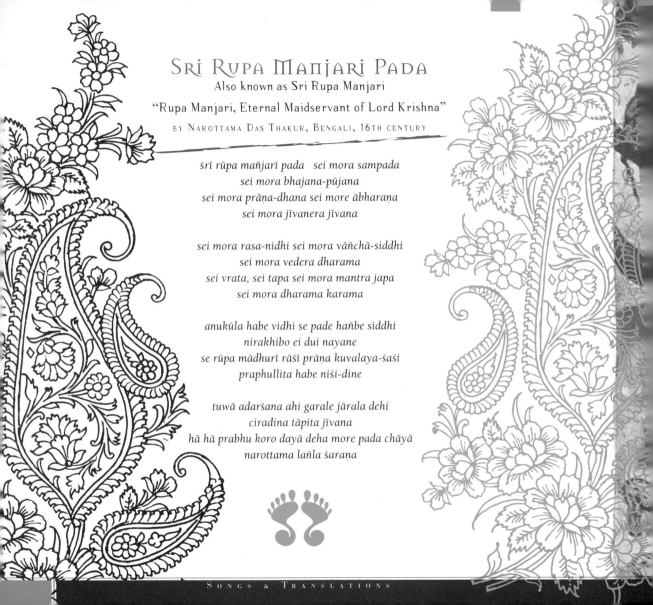

SONGS & TRANSLATIONS

Sri Rupa Manjari Pada
TRANSLATION

Sri Rupa Manjari's lotus feet are my only possession. They are my religious practice, my worship. They are my wealth; they are my ornament, the life of my life.

They are my treasure house of sacred rapture, they are the fulfillment of my deepest wishes, they are my prescribed duty. They are my religious vow; they are my austerities, my meditation and my mantra. They are my religious obligation.

One day, fate will smile upon me and I will be perfected in a position of service to her. I will see that form which is an ocean of sweetness, which will cause the moon lotus of my heart to bloom night and day.

The snake of separation from you spits venom that burns my body. I have long suffered in this life. O my lord! Please be merciful and give me the shade of Your lotus feet. Narottam has taken shelter of You.

Sri Nrisingha Pranam

Also known as Nrisingha Prayers

"Prayers to Sri Nrisingha"

ONE

namas te narasimhāya
prahlādāhlāda-dāyine
hiraṇyakaśipor vakṣaḥ-
śilā-ṭaṅka-nakhālaye

ito nṛsimhaḥ parato nṛsimho
yato yato yāmi tato nṛsimhaḥ
bahir nṛsimho hṛdaye nṛsimho
nṛsimham ādim śaraṇam prapadye

TWO

Prayer to Lord Nrisingha

BY JAYADEVA GOSWAMI, SANSKRIT, 12TH CENTURY

tava kara-kamala-vare nakham adbhuta-śṛṅgam
dalita-hiraṇyakaśipu-tanu-bhṛṅgam
keśava dhṛta-nara-hari-rūpa jaya jagad-īśa hare

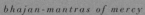

Sri Nrisingha Pranam

TRANSLATION

ONE

I offer my obeisances to Lord Nrisingha Deva, who gives joy to Prahlad Maharaja and whose nails are like chisels on the stone-like chest of Hiranyakashipu. Lord Nrisingha is here and also there. Wherever I go Lord Nrisingha is there. He is in the heart and is outside as well. I surrender to Lord Nrisingha, the origin of all things and the supreme refuge.

TWO

O Keshava! O lord of the universe! O Lord Hari who has assumed the form of a half-man, half-lion! All glories to you! With the wonderfully sharp nails on your beautiful lotus hands You have ripped apart the wasp-like body of Hiranyakashipu.

Sri-Guru-vandana

Also known as Sri Guru

Prayers to Sri Guru

by Narottam Das Thakur, Bengali, 16th century

śrī-guru-caraṇa-padma kevala bhakati-sadma
bandoṅ mui sābadhāna mote
jāṅhāra prasāde bhāi e bhava toriyā jāi
kṛṣṇa-prāpti hoy jāṅhā hoite

guru-mukha-padma-bākya cittete koriyā aikya
āra nā koriho mone āśā
śrī guru caraṇe rati, ei se uttama gati
je prasāde pūre sarva āśā

cakhu-dāna dilo jei janme janme prabhu sei
divya-jñāna hṛde prakāśito
prema bhakti jāṅhā hoite avidyā-vināśa jāte
vede gāya jāṅhāra carito

śrī-guru-karuṇā-sindhu adhama-janāra bandhu
lokanātha lokera jīvan
hā hā prabhu koro doyā deho more pada-chāyā
ebe joś ghusuk tribhuvan

Sri-Guru-vandana
TRANSLATION

I worship the spiritual master's lotus feet, the abode of exclusive devotion, with great care and attention. O brother, by his mercy one can cross over this material state of being and through him one can reach Krishna.

Fix your mind on the words emanating from the lotus mouth of the spiritual master. Place your hopes in nothing else. Affection for the guru's lotus feet is the ultimate goal, for by his mercy all of one's aspirations are realized.

The one who gave me eyes to see is my master, birth after birth. By his grace, the light of divine knowledge illuminates my heart. From him comes ecstatic love for Krishna; from him, ignorance is destroyed and so the scriptures glorify his deeds.

The spiritual master is the ocean of compassion, the friend of the lowly. He is the lord and life of the worlds. O Master! Be merciful and give me shelter in the shade of your lotus feet. May your glories be sung throughout the universe.

(Narottam Das, *Prema Bhakti Chandrika*)

Govindam

"Hymn to Govinda, the Primeval Lord"
FROM THE BRAHMA SAMHITA

govindam ādi-puruṣaṁ tam ahaṁ bhajāmi
veṇuṁ kvaṇantam aravinda-dalāyatākṣam-
barhāvataṁsam asitāmbuda-sundarāṅgam
kandarpa-koṭi-kamanīya-viśeṣa-śobhaṁ
govindam ādi-puruṣaṁ tam ahaṁ bhajāmi

aṅgāni yasya sakalendriya-vṛtti-manti
paśyanti pānti kalayanti ciraṁ jaganti
ānanda-cinmaya-sad-ujjvala-vigrahasya
govindam ādi-puruṣaṁ tam ahaṁ bhajāmi

with blooming
eyes like lotus
petals, His
head decked
with peacock
feathers,
the figure of
beauty tinged
with the hue
of blue clouds,
His unique
loveliness
charming
millions of
cupids.

I worship Govinda, the primeval Lord, who is adept in playing on His flute, with blooming eyes like lotus petals, His head decked with peacock feathers, the figure of beauty tinged with the hue of blue clouds, His unique loveliness charming millions of cupids.

I worship Govinda, the primeval Lord, whose transcendental form is full of bliss, truth, substantiality and is thus full of the most dazzling splendor. Each of the limbs of that transcendental figure possesses in Himself, the full-fledged functions of all the organs, and eternally sees, maintains and manifests the infinite universes, both spiritual and mundane.

I worship Govinda, the primeval Lord, whose transcendental form is full of bliss, truth, substantiality and is thus full of the most dazzling splendor.

AN INTERVIEW WITH KIM WATERS AND HANS CHRISTIAN BY N. D. KOSTER

Lord Chaitanya did not advent Himself to liberate only a few men of India. Rather, His main objective was to emancipate all living entities of all countries throughout the entire universe and preach the Eternal Religion. Lord Chaitanya says in the *Chaitanya Bhagavata*: "In every town, country and village, My name will be sung." There is no doubt that this unquestionable order will come to pass. Very soon the unparalleled path of Harinam sankirtan will be propagated all over the world. Already we are seeing the symptoms. — Bhaktivinode Thakur

Q: You've chosen to sing and adapt melodies from a fairly obscure musical tradition, that of Gaudiya Vaishnavism. How is it that you became inspired to do so?

HANS I was first inspired by Kim's renditions of these songs. Her sublime voice and innate musicality spoke to me clearly, and I had wanted to produce music like this for a long time. Perhaps the simplicity of the melodies and the beauty of the languages were the teasers, and an additional inspiration was the lyrics themselves. Before I even knew what tradition this material was based on I was intrigued by

Clearly we have tapped into a tradition that deserves the greatest respect because people with the highest aspirations have composed and performed these songs.

it, and subsequent exploration showed me that there was a universal quality to it that I could relate to very well. This, in turn, is very compatible with our intention to create music where the messages, the sounds, the melodies all come together to create a powerful experience. The material that we work with provides a wealth of inspiration for this purpose.

KIM My first exposure to the Vaishnava tradition was in the early 70's when I had the good fortune of coming in contact with His Divine Grace A. C. Bhaktivedanta Swami Prabhupada and some of his early western students. Traveling to various temples, I began to meet a very diverse group of people who were all attracted to this rather exotic spiritual movement from India. Prabhupada had brought to the western world not only a spiritual movement, but also an aesthetic one. The various artistic forms of expression made possible through this ancient tradition—whether it was through music, painting, dance, drama, cuisine or the refined art of deity worship—provided a new vehicle for many people to express themselves not only as spiritual seekers, but also as artists. As much as some may have tried to follow this path in a traditional manner (which was definitely recommended), there was an unavoidable blending of eastern and western styles to some degree. A very unique movement in art was born at this time and still continues to thrive.

Q It is stated in the Vedic literatures that mantra has a purifying and transforming effect. Is this something you've encountered in your own lives? What do you hear from your listeners regarding their experiences with the music and mantras?

> You cannot see Me with your present eyes. Therefore I give you divine eyes, so that you can behold My mystic opulence. — Bhagavad Gita

HANS Yes, I have experienced a transformative effect since working with this material, but transformation comes hand in hand with creativity for me. Even prior to Rasa I had transformative experiences while working on my solo recordings (*Phantoms* and *Surrender* being the two most recent). As a matter of fact, my creative explorations always brought me to a spiritual realm, a place of surrender to and recognition of a Divine Being. In the process of "getting there," of working creatively, one burns a lot of personal garbage and goes through purification. Now, imagine combining this process with sacred mantras and devotional bhajans: the potency for transformation increases dramatically. That's why Rasa's music seems to transform many people's lives. We are getting testimony from our audiences nationwide that their lives have

been transformed by our music, sometimes dramatically. A lot of healing experiences have been associated with Rasa's music, and several people with terminal illness have chosen to die to our music. We are extremely humbled by these responses.

KIM Meeting Bhaktivedanta Swami Prabhupada in person and discovering this yoga

of love through him and his teachings was so inspiring and such a rare gift. I couldn't help but want to do whatever possible to pay back and honor that gift. It was at that time that I began illustrating a selection of verses from his translation of the Bhagavad Gita. I also began listening to and singing with recordings of these wonderful songs and

gradually delved deeper into their actual meanings. I started to immerse myself in these hauntingly beautiful melodies and began to discover the depths of the extraordinary souls whose hearts these songs emanated from. Many of the songs are spiritual cries for mercy and often they would bring me to tears. Singing them became a great source of solace and a way to pray. It seemed they would bring me to a very deep place within myself, where I actually would feel closer to God. Realizing that Divine presence and mercy had a healing effect that was a very transforming experience for me. Painting and illustrating sacred images and singing and listening to this material are ways for me to stay in touch with that experience.

The sacred nature of these songs and mantras makes it a very powerful and humbling experience to present this music in the form of Rasa. The response from our audience has been overwhelming. We have received many messages from people all over the world who've been truly inspired and sometimes even healed by it. Initially I had some concern that those whom may be more purist in attitude might find fault in the non-traditional freedom of artistic expression we've taken. But I am relieved and delighted

the Divine expresses itself uniquely through every living entity

to find that there is great room for individual expression, and with the right heart, we can inspire and encourage each other. One of the aspects of Vaishnava philosophy that has always appealed to me is the emphasis that we are all individual spirit souls and that the Divine expresses itself uniquely through every living entity. Although I'm not an initiated disciple, I truly wish to honor Bhaktivedanta Swami Prabhupada to whatever degree I am able and in the most beautiful way possible. I deeply appreciate all the encouragement from the wonderful devotees of this extraordinary tradition, and I am proud to call them my friends. Prabhupada himself also gave me a great blessing while seeing my illustrated Bhagavad Gita when he said: "You are introducing a new art form to this country—you will receive great rewards for this. Do it!"

Q. After performing these songs for some years now, do you see an evolution in your own thinking about them?

HANS I have come to love them more and more as I learn more about them. Clearly we have tapped into a tradition that deserves the greatest respect because people with the highest aspirations have composed and performed these songs. They are like polished crystals that you hold in your hands, spreading the light. I think that people want to hear these songs, are moved by their meanings, and resonate with our renditions of them. I can see a universal quality in their

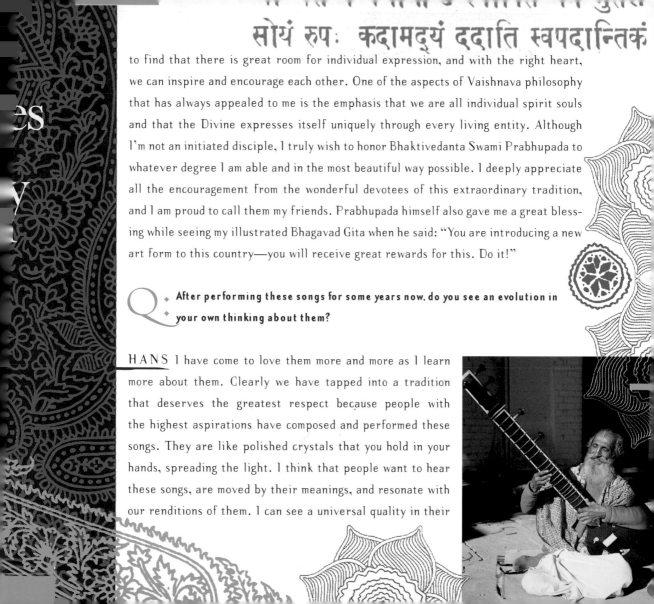

meanings that transcends cultural and religious identities. This is why they work so well even within our style of music.

Q: How would you like Rasa to be understood? How do you view it?

HANS & KIM We hope that people will embrace Rasa for what it is—a creative expression of traditional spiritual bhajans. Our intention is come up with interesting new renditions of these sacred songs, and this effort usually deviates from established traditional lines. We see Rasa as a catalyst that introduces our Western audiences to sacred material from the Vaishnava tradition, and by doing so opens their hearts and minds to the universal qualities of love and compassion for one another. As Kim and I explore and express ourselves creatively within the framework of this tradition, we hope to open doors for our listeners to have profound and positive experiences in their own lives. Nothing could make us happier.

> I can see a universal quality in their meanings that transcends cultural and religious identities.

Instruments

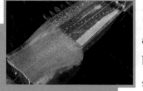

Sarangi—The sarangi is a bowed Indian fiddle with a goat skin top that is played with the cuticles of the left hand. It has three main strings and thirty-six resonating strings that are grouped into four different tuned sets. Unlike the sitar or sarod, which were played at the courts of medieval Indian nobility, the sarangi is considered a folklore instrument and has been primarily utilized as vocal accompaniment. Its popularity has declined as the aforementioned instruments gained more and more recognition. The instrument used on this recording was built by Ricki Ram in New Delhi and modified by Hans Christian.

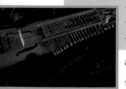

Nyckelharpa—The nyckelharpa is a bowed Scandinavian key fiddle with four main strings and 12 resonating strings. The player pushes a set of wooden keys that in turn press against the strings. The origins of the nyckelharpa extend back to the Middle Ages, where it shares a common ancestry with another folk instrument, the hurdy gurdy.

Sitara—The sitara is a miniature version of the Indian sitar, with curved brass frets, four play strings, eight resonating strings, and two arched bridges that create the characteristic buzzing sound. The particular instrument played by Hans is custom made from solid ebony by a San Francisco Bay area instrument maker.

Harmonium—The harmonium originates in Germany and England. It became popular with immigrant pioneers while traveling west in the US. It was also brought to India by the British. It was quickly absorbed into Indian music culture, admired for its drone quality and portability, but was not considered a traditional Indian instrument. Only in the last century has the harmonium found its way into traditional Indian music.

Udu—The udu is a claypot drum. This drum can be found in different cultures,

including African and Indian, and is being made in great variations by instrument makers worldwide. Its unique characteristic lies in its design: two openings in a pear shaped clay drum that allow the player to dramatically bend the pitch of the drum by covering the holes. Some udus even have an animal skin stretched across one of the holes to give them more of a drum sound. Many of the low drum sounds on this CD were played on an udu.

Mridanga—The word mridanga can be translated as "mrid," meaning clay, and "anga," meaning limb. It is constructed of clay limbs.

The mridanga is a rare instrument with a unique history. There are a few schools of mridanga still being conducted today. Their lineages trace back to Gadahara Pandit, Srinivasa Acharya and Narottam Dasa. These schools are known as Manharshayi, Mandarani and Garanhati respectively. There are very few teachers left who are still practicing this sacred drumming tradition in its original form.

Some of these representatives say that the mridanga, as we know it now, was brought into being when Sri Chaitanya ordered his associates to construct clay drums instead of the heavy and costly wooden drums. It's birth was thus connected to the cultural and spiritual revolution of sixteenth century Bengal.

In fact, the Manaharshayi school tells the story of Lord Krishna's flute pleading not to be left behind when he incarnated as Sri Chaitanya. During this period, Krishna was accompanied by his flute in the form of the mridanga.

CD CREDITS

Kabe Habe Bolo
Kim Waters- vocals
Hans Christian- cello, sarangi, bass, bells
& shakers, frame drum,
keyboards & textures
Girish Gambira- tablas
Alan Kozlowski- hamsa vina

Samsara
Kim Waters- vocals, tambura
Hans Christian- sitara, tambura, cello, bass,
keyboards & textures
Girish Gambira- udu, tablas
John Loose- shakers, hihat

Hari Haraye
Kim Waters- vocals, tambura
Hans Christian- sarangi, bass,
keyboards & textures
Girish Gambira- mridangam, udu
John Loose- kanjira, triangle, cabasa,
maraca, shakers
Robert Powell- electric and acoustic guitars

Sri Rupa Manjari
Kim Waters- vocals
Hans Christian- nyckelharpa, bass, cello,
keyboards & textures
Girish Gambira- udu, talking drums, mridangam
John Loose- ghatam, shakers& bells

Nrisingha Prayers
Kim Waters- vocals, tambura, bells
Hans Christian- sarangi, bass, bells,
keyboards & textures
Girish Gambira- tablas, udu, kanjira

Sri Guru
Kim Waters- vocals, tambura, percussion
Hans Christian- sitara, cello, bass, kartals,
keyboards & textures
Girish Gambira- udu, tabla, morcheng (mouth harp)
John Loose- ambient percussion, kanjira,
dumbek, shakers, hihat
John Wubbenhorst- bansouri flute

Govindam Prayers
Kim Waters- vocals
Yamuna Devi- guest vocals
Hans Christian- cello, sitara, bass, harmonium, bells,
keyboards & textures
Girish Gambira- mridangam, spring drum, morcheng
John Loose- ghatam, kartals, shakers, tambourine
Bhima Karma- kartals

Acknowledgments

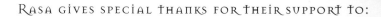

Rasa gives special thanks for their support to:

Raoul Goff, Navadwip Koster and everyone at Mandala Publishing; Stephen & Leyla Hill, Jeff Klein, Yamuna and Dina, Radhika Sarin, Mukunda Maharaja, Rukmini, Gauravani Buchwald, Madhava Maharaja, Tridandi Maharaja, Narasingha Maharaja, Ramesh Sawhney, Stephen Jarvis, Alan Kozlowski and Sandra Hay, Henry Schoellkopf, Davey and Chris Murray, and our families in Washington DC and Germany.

Thanks to the musicians for their superb playing.

In loving memory of George Harrison.
This recording is dedicated to A. C. Bhaktivedanta Swami Prabhupada.
May it inspire many souls....

Produced and engineered by Hans Christian
Musical arrangements by Hans Christian and Kim Waters

Recorded and mixed at Allemande Music, Fairfax, California
Additional recording by Doug Perry at Perry's Recording Studio, Kamloops, B. C.
Arrangements copyright 2001 Allemande Music/bmi
Administered by Liminal Music/bmi

Mastering Bob Ohlsson and Stephen Hill at Hearts of Space, Sausalito, California.

Bengali and sanskrit translation and biographical research and writing by Jan Brzezinski
Instrument photos by Neil Greentree, courtesy of Hearts of Space Records
Editing, introduction, artist photographs and interview by ND Koster

For more information on Swami B.B. Tirtha visit www.gokul.org

For more information on Swami B.V. Tripurari visit www.swami.org

✝Rack List

1 Kabe Habe Bolo

2 Samsara *(Sri Sri Gurvaṣṭaka)*

3 Hari Haraye *(Nama Sankirtan)*

4 Sri Rupa Manjari

5 Prayers to Sri Nrisingha *(Sri Nrisingha Pranama)*

6 Sri Guru *(Sri-Guru-vandana)*

7 Govindam

परं सर्वात्मस्नपनं परं विजयते श्रीकृष्णसङ्कीर्तनम् सर्वात्मस्नपन

बहुधा नाम्नामकारि बहुधा निजसर्वशक्ति- नाम्नामकारि नाम्नामक

र्पिताः स्त्रार्पिता नियमितः स्मरणे न कालःभगवन्ममापिस्त्रार्पि

कृपा एतादृशी तव कृपा भगवन्ममापि भगवन्ममापि नाम्नामक

हाजनि दुर्दैवमीदृशमिहाजनि नानुरागःतव भगवन्ममाज्ञिआनन्दाम्बु

चेन तृणादपि सुनीचेन तरोरिव सहिष्णुना सहिष्णुना नाम्नामका

नदेन अमानिना मानदेन कीर्तनीयः सदा हरिः सदा आनन्दाम्बुधिव

नं न स् न धनं न जनं न सुन्दरीं कामये कीर्तनीय सदा हरिः स्त्र

जगदीश कवितां वा जगदीशः कामये सदाजन्मनीश्वरे आनन्दाम्बु

जन्मनि मम जन्मनि जन्मनीश्वरे मां विषमे भवाम्बधौ सदा ह

हैतुकी भवताद्भक्तिरहैतुकी त्वयिविषमे भवाम्बुधौभवताद्भक्तिरहैतु

ज! अयि नन्दतनुज! किङ्करं किङ्करं अयि नन्दतनुज!मम जन्मनि

षमे पतितं मां विषमे भवाम्बुधौ मां विषमे भवाम्बुधौ सदा हरि

पादपड कृपया तव पादपङ्कज- अयि अयि विचिन्तय आनन्द

मस्तपनं परं विजयते श्रीकृष्णसङ्कीर्तनम् सर्वात्मस्नपनं सर्वात्मस्

नकारि बहुधा निजसर्वशक्ति- नाम्नामकारि नाम्नामकारि नाम्नामक

र्पिता नियमितः स्मरणे न कालःभगवन्ममापि स्तत्रार्पिता स्तत्रार्पि

शी तव कृपा भगवन्ममापि भगवन्ममापि नाम्नामकारि एतादृशी

मीहृशमिहाजनि नानुरागःतव भगवन्ममाज्ञिआनन्दाम्बुधिव दुर्दैवमीह

पि सुनीचेन तरोरिव सहिष्णुना सहिष्णुना नाम्नामकारि तृणादपि

नेना मानदेन कीर्तनीय सदा हरिः सदा आनन्दाम्बुधिव अमानिना

ने न जनं न सुन्दरीं कामये कीर्तनीय सदा हरिः स्तत्रार्पिता न धनं न

तां वा जगदीशः कामये सदा जन्मनीश्वरे आनन्दाम्बुधिव कविता ह

जन्मनि जन्मनीश्वरे मां विषमे भवाम्बुधौ सदा हरिः मम जन्म

द्भक्तिरहैतुकी त्वयिविषमे भवाम्बुधैवताद्भक्तिरहैतुकी भवताद्भ

नन्दतनुज! किङ्करं किङ्करं अयि नन्दतनुज!मम जन्मनि अयि नन्द

मां विषमे भवाम्बुधौ मां विषमे भवाम्बुधौ सदा हरिःपतितं मा

न तव पादपङ्कज- अयि अयि विचिन्तय आनन्दाम्बुधिव कृपया